Proud and on My Feet

Proud and on My Feet

POEMS BY
J. W. RIVERS

For Arlene Jones: I kiss madam's finger tips, hands and forearms; to kiss elbows is gauche. Your servant, Esterházy

Athens
The University of Georgia Press

Copyright © 1983 by J. W. Rivers
Published by the University of Georgia Press
Athens, Georgia 30602

Set in 10 on 12 point Monticello type

The paper in this book meets the guidelines for permanence
and durability of the Committee on Production Guidelines for
Book Longevity of the Council on Library Resources.

Printed in the United States of America

Library of Congress Cataloging in Publication Data

Rivers, J. W. (Jim W.)
    Proud and on my feet.

    I. Title.
PS3568.I832P7   811'.54   82-4768
ISBN 0-8203-0632-0   AACR2
ISBN 0-8203-0633-9 (pbk.)

The publication of this book is supported by a grant from the
National Endowment for the Arts, a federal agency.

For Mercedes and Francis

Acknowledgments

To James R. Scrimgeour and Robert D. Sutherland, editors, Pikestaff Publications—good friends, tough critics. Many of the Chicago poems in this book were featured in *Pikestaff Review*. Several of the poems in parts two and three of this book appear in *Pikestaff Forum*. To Jack and Betty Weaver, Susan Ludvigson, Arla Holroyd, and Grace Freeman— good human beings who share with me a love of poetry. To David Pichaske, editor, Spoon River Press—for poems that appeared in a chapbook entitled *from the Chicago Notebook: Memories of the South Side*. And to Ann Deagon, warm and supportive always.

To the following periodicals in which poems in this book have appeared or will appear, some of them in slightly altered form: *The Akros Review, Antenna, Coraddi, The Davidson Miscellany, The Devil's Millhopper, The Greensboro Review, The Hiram Poetry Review, Kudzu, The London Magazine, The Maelstrom Review, Maize, The Mid-American Review, The New Mexico Humanities Review, Puerto del Sol, The Red Cedar Review, Riversedge, San Fernando Poetry Journal, The South Carolina Review, Spoon River Quarterly, The Sun* (Chapel Hill, N.C.), and *Tar River Poetry*. "Tonsillectomy" is included in the *1981 Anthology of Magazine Verse and Yearbook of American Poetry*. A selection from part three of this book will appear this year in a broadside to be released by Watermark Press.

J.W.R.

Contents

I

from The Chicago Notebook: Memories of the South Side

Oh, to be a shaver again, playing like these kids, stealing coal from the railroad yards.

JAMES T. FARRELL
Judgment Day

January Morning

Old Man Winter's on a hell-bender
in his glad rags,
drops his load like a B-17
with a plaster of Paris virus,
turns the fire hydrant into a monster
my dog can't cock a good leg at.
You'd lose your balls
on the golf course
if you were nuts enough to be there.
Smoke looks like dark popsicles
stuck in chimneys.
I think I'll go inside
and sit on the radiator;
this cold can freeze a drunk's insides,
you can build an igloo
with blocks of antifreeze.
I can break your jaw with my mitten.

Shoveling Snow in Chicago

The den of a squirrel
would be perfect for you,
a love feast of acorns
above the snow and slush:
you could toss the shells
anyplace you please,
gorge yourself to heart's content,
sleep all day, not have to go
to science class
to look at mud daubers
or dumb lima beans.

The only people on the block
who have to move
tons and tons
of snow and slush
are certain little boys
with mortal allergies
to splintery shovel handles
but the doctor
won't tell their parents
because he knows as doctors know
just who pays the bills.

These little boys
will grow up to become doctors,
maybe even fathers,
will prescribe acorn rest
in squirrel nest beds
for other afflicted little boys,

and snow and slush in big doses
and heavy-handled shovels
for their grandparents
and for dumb giggly girls.

Late at Night in the Kitchen

The cookies are for the holidays.

Into the kitchen
we move
on puppy dog feet.
Ma will have kittens
if she hears us grunt
by the fat pig
of a cookie jar.
She'll spring
out of bed
like a mousetrap,
chase us all over
her Johnson Wax floor,
let us have it
on the behind
with her wooden mixing spoon
as we squeal
and scurry like roaches
surprised in the night.

Making Cakes and Dumplings

My picture puzzle is small enough
to sit on the kitchen table yet
leave room for Aunt Josie
to roll dough for Rákóczy cake,
but when she makes palacsinta
she has to pull the dough
to the edges of the table
so it's thinner than Kleenex
or toilet paper, and I have
to put my almost done
picture puzzle on the floor.

Jars and cups and plates
from the old country, full
of morello cherries and poppy seed,
grated lemon rind, walnuts,
cottage cheese and sour cream
all the way from Maxwell Street
are on the counter, and semolina
dumplings are boiling already
on the gas stove for supper.

Uncle Oscar gives me a hammer
from the tool room to smash walnuts
into ingredient-sized pieces
but if he cracks a tooth
or splices a gum on a shell
in the cake I never again for a month
get into the men only tool room,
he says, or wash my hands with soap
in the can from Death Valley
that Wallace Beery uses,

or get more puzzles of PT boats
sinking the Japanese fleet.

As I pound walnuts into VJ Day
and see my boats at general quarters
I drop cherry-pit bombs
and walnut shells on the Japs.

On a Mulberry Tree Branch in Jackson Park

The U-505 at the Museum
can't dive far or fast enough
to escape your radar vision,
you scout the Crib
far out in the lake,
see clear to the Loop on drizzly days,
hear kidneys mash, bones crack
at Mount Carmel spring football,
know the score
and what inning they're in
at the schoolyard softball game
all the way over in Elmhurst.

The secret's in the berries,
disguised as baby hand grenades.
If Mrs. Dalton ate just one
she'd know you're not in school today
or even in her music class.
But she can't know the berries
let you be where you're not,
they cast a mulberry spell
on music teachers so they park
their brains in bass clef
and sing and think off key.

The cloak of invisibility
starts on the lowest branch,
goes up with you and the growing point
until someday you're free to go unseen
among fighter pilots and birds.

The Non-Swimmer Advises His Nephew about the Beach

Don't go in Lake Michigan
at night, Uncle Oscar says.
Don't even walk the beach.
Things worse than gypsies
with blood-red bandannas
and blood-red butcher knives
come from the bottom,
seize you with tentacles,
crush you in claws,
suck blood from your heart.

Don't go in daytime either.
The sun peels your skin
like a bear strips a lamb.
Bad people steal your money
and pee on your clothes
while you're in the water
stepping on broken glass.
The lake sucks your blood
and you're dead
before you drown.

From Burnside to Goldblatt's by Streetcar

You're only really safe in Burnside,
Right here in Hungarian Village, Uncle Oscar
Lets you know before your first streetcar solo
From 94th and Cottage Grove to 63rd and Halstead
To see Ma during break at Goldblatt's Department Store:

Keep an eye out for Jews
who'll snatch your underwear,
Poles who'll take
your Tom Mix whistling ring,
finger and all, and your
Captain Midnight secret decoder;
the Italian neighborhood
is so hot it can blow any second
like a Chicago pineapple;
those Germans brained two nurses
and a nun just last Sunday;
the Japanese carve kids
with swords from head to toe,
toss pieces on front doorsteps
with the milk and morning paper;
the chocolate drops from Africa
blow poison darts with rusty barbs,
steal your change, streetcar transfers
and baseball cards, dance around
as you lie dying forever;
if and when you get to Halstead Street
watch for Mongolian perverts
under manhole covers,
Armenians in the awning
with deadly piano wire,

avoid basements and Ukranians
with beards and damp knives.

And you wonder just how much you need a chocolate soda
At the soda fountain with Ma
During break at Goldblatt's Department Store.

Late to School

If the tardy bell rings on you
one day without a note
the Truant Officer knows,
stirs among her coffee and clipboards.

Two tardy slips:
she stretches, flicks her tongue,
glides from the attendance office
into the hall of justice.

Aunt Josie doesn't write notes
in English,
never went to school in Chicago,
teacher can't read in Hungarian.

Late three times and the law
bites into your record
that follows you from fifth grade
all your life everywhere you go
never lets you loose
can't get a job
get married
have kids
own a dump truck
rent a hotel room
because you're late
        late
          late.

Tonsillectomy

The doctor's aseptic popsicle stick
from his tongue-depressor jar
is into your mouth and past your teeth
before you can yell shazam.
His evil beady yellow eyes
dance on a probing flashlight ray,
invade your mouth and inspect your throat
all the way down to the neck.
The boy's tonsils have to go
you overhear him say, and you're
Billy Batson with no lightning bolt,
Buck Rogers without his flying belt,
Red Ryder minus his horse.
Better off trapped on an asteroid
with no food or rocket fuel
or in a chapter of *Jungle Tales*
on an island of killer ants
than strapped like a dog
to a hospital table
with Doctor Ming at your throat.

You wake up silent in a ward
among the tongueless dead
with your mouth cut out
and your throat slit through
all the way down to your neck.
You look around for the ether bomb
that blew you into space,
find only a slithering galactic squid
posing as a nurse:
it wants you to eat a plateful
of strawberry star saliva,

and you know by heart the secret rules
of the space ranger commando kit—
if you eat so much as a half a drop
you turn into a giant dwarf.
Before its slimy tentacle
gets the strawberry goo to your face,
you press a hidden nerve in your wrist
and completely disappear.

The Training of a Fighter

Gerald McKee is after you, says he'll sit on your head,
Make you eat all the gravel in the schoolyard;
Sam Finlay and Jerry Koupal are after you too,
Going to hang you by their patrol belts
From Tribune Tower; and Big Top the Bully says
He'll toss you piece by piece into a Stockyard gutter.

But Uncle Oscar's going to help you:

Eat poppy seed cake and pörkölt,
what Matyas Corvinus ate
to fight the Turk;
do chins on the awning bar,
shovel coal to get in shape,
coat yourself with coal dust
and you will be a Fekete Sereg
fighter against the Turk.

Jab with the left,
knee to the crotch,
finish them off with the roll
of pennies to the jaw;
strike like Kossuth Apánk struck,
strike for your self-respect.

If they make you bleed
blind them with your blood,
if they break your bones
turn your bones into clubs,
if they bite off your ears
rip out their eyes.

They will not throw you into the gutter.
You will throw them into the Danube.
You will come home bloody,
you will come home hurt,
you will come home with your ears torn.
You will come home proud on your feet.

Hardball

Slow-pitch is for sissies,
you find, when you show off
your sixteen-inch softball
and your friends split their seams.
The Pros play hardball:
go to Wrigley Field or Comiskey,
see if you ever see a softball.
Do you ever see softballers
on bubblegum cards?
Smoke Camels on billboards?
Shave with Gillettes?
You find after summers, years,
of slow-pitch, it ruins your eye,
arm, reflexes, and all the rest.
You think of scraped knuckles and knees,
raw shins, the bottle cap in your neck
that time you slid into second,
sun and dust in your eyes,
flung bats, popsicle stick caps,
bricks or branches for bases,
and you pack your birthday ball
into its box, thinking how
you've wasted eye, arm, reflexes,
summers, years, and all the rest.

Valentine

From across the room
a Valentine from Mary Fung.
You never took her
for serious before,
she never hung her wrap
on your hook in the cloak room.
You stare at her across the aisles,
see only the outer shell
of an oriental pearl.
Too late to send her a card
of construction paper and paste;
maybe some cinnamon hearts tomorrow,
or ask her to climb your favorite tree
over in Jackson Park.
Maybe she can't climb trees
or sit on handlebars,
maybe Chinese girls only win
spelling bees and eat noodles
on the floor. But when
Gerald McKee at recess
teases her to tears
for chop suey English
and sneaky slanty eyes
you pitch gravel
into his tenement mouth,
don't give a dime for the rest of his face
or a Chinaman's chance for his life.
She gives you a smile like the Texas border,
and you wonder if she likes
orange popsicles better,
or lemon.

Sunday Morning Sandlot Football

I watched you guys go through that signal practice. You stunk!
If you go into this game like that, it'll be the Fort Dearborn
massacre.

JAMES T. FARRELL
The Young Manhood of Studs Lonigan

The Scotties came in cars.

They never go to church,
must be at least nineteen
(why aren't they in the Marines?)
not one of them without a beard
or hair on his arms
clear down to his hands.

Only the quarterback
looks our age—
has a tattoo on his chest,
smokes Pall Malls,
warms up with a bottle of Schlitz
and big bites of blood sausage.

Those linemen look like Merchandise Mart,
better an end run around Navy Pier.

They've got girl friends,
beer on ice,
cigarettes,
kidney pads.
We've got one substitute:
his parents
took him to church today.

To Uncle Oscar, Dead of Lung Cancer

It gives no sign; no sibyl
Contrives to trace its filaments
As with Penelope's constancy
It weaves among the trees
Cocoons of silk and wax.
It is, it does,
But does not see itself;
It lives, it grows,
Has no fingers or feet,
Yet plies with pudding patience
The butter paths it probes.
Resistance melts to this siege
Of cocoons; sap blends with silk
And wax in a flow of fraternal pledge,
Graceful encounter on inroads
Where branches murmur
The biographies of their cells.

Such tactics serve in all wars,
But even sandbox warfare
Has its deranged officials
Who order a pressing ahead.
Little silkworm point men
Metastasize to attention:
Outposts must be taken,
The forest felled,
Prisoners wasted.

II

from The Scattered Poems
of Esterházy

Farewell, dear God, I'm leaving for America.

ESTERHÁZY
Diary of a Magyar

The Esterházy Family Picnic
Hungary, 1929

I've heard that the dead make no noise.
Father was like that until today
but now he talks even to Sasha the frog,
who's buried in a bowl of potato salad
to escape the July heat.

Father talks to keep from hearing Sándor Nagy,
who tells of being attacked
in the Black Forest by Nibelungen.
Father says he'd like to have a spear,
creep beneath that loudmouth Nagy,
thrust it into his ass hair.

Paprika gets into Sasha's eyes,
he springs from the bowl.
No one is surprised that salad
scatters like manna, which according to Father
was only matzo balls.

Sándor leapfrogs after Sasha into Lake Balaton.

Aunt Malvin peels more potatoes.
Aunt Josie grinds paprika fruit.
Uncle Oscar scours the lake
for frogs for frog soup.
Father sharpens a stick.

Esterházy Shakes His Fist at the Sunday Sky:
A Study in Chiaroscuro
Chicago, 1950

> Lord! It is me standing out here
> on this prairie!
>
> NED RANDLE

Lord! I'm standing here
on the roof of the three flat!
The sky is a glare of South Chicago
steel mills, a chemical sunset
you never intended not even for Gary.
The family went to Phil Schmidt's in Hammond
this afternoon for fried chicken
but had to come back—
black rain fell as we stood in line.
Now the wind brings a huge fist of a cloud
toward me on Harper Avenue.
I yell, raise my own fist,
brace for an electric rapier:
death of the hero, outlined in fire,
but only some white shit falls
from startled pigeons.

Esterházy on Mount Everest
May 25, 1953

The Sherpa guides have given up.
I see them far below around a fire
eating imported rhinoceros meat, hear them
slurp their tea with yak butter.
After a month of climbing
they refuse to come farther
because of one pawmark in the snow. But I,
who've crossed the Hindu Kush many times
alone, continue.
I've no fear of the Yeti.

My camp is five hundred
feet from the top, four days in advance
of Hillary and his guide. Those two
are waiting for morning.
I launch my final assault
tonight.
It's snowing
as I start up the sheer wall. The moon,
a dimpled peasant woman who wears no babushka,
is blotted out.
I arrive after midnight.

Hello,
says the voice of Sándor Nagy.
His little Russian frog Sasha
hops on my frozen beard and kisses me.
Want a cup of Spanish chocolate?
Or do you prefer hot borscht?

Esterházy and the Swimmer
Rock Hill, South Carolina, 1963

She drives me mad
across the YMCA pool.
The sun kindles her hair
into Titian's dream.
I want to dive with her
into a Tahitian pond,
come up in a secret grotto.
The watch within my wrist
says *now*, when all the youth
I ever had is here.

She strokes through warm
intimate water, stands wet
before me head to foot,
offers her breath,
her eyes, her vibes,
the way she pulls off
her suit in our cave
behind the waterfall.

Esterházy and the Cat Woman

Your eyes prowl the dark,
twin butterflies that hunt
by night. You stretch,
arch your back, your tongue
touches my lips,
darts into my mouth.
Come to me. Come
to the Esterházy of cool nose
and concealed claws.

The Office Suite Sequence, 1965

Esterházy in His Chicago Office

I look down at Prudential Building
from the Esterházy Corporate Suite.
Navy Pier is a toothpick on the lake.

Something's in my bloodstream.

Agnes the new secretary comes in without knocking,
startles my synaptic reflexes.
My toes grow numb, my lips tremble;
paralysis creeps into my diaphragm and chest muscles.

It's shellfish poison from butter clams, she says;
it was on those envelopes you licked,

in the New York strip you ate for lunch,
even in your Listerine.

She polishes her nails.

After Hours in the Office

I pet Fair-Haired Boy the piranha
who playfully nips my hand in his wall-to-wall tank.

Far below on the lake a small-craft warning is in effect,
a summer thunderstorm rages
at the eightieth floor of the Corporate Parking Lot.
I make a note to assemble a squall management team.

Agnes thumbs through my statistical analysis charts,
with a camera in her left breast she photographs data
on improved alfalfa tolerance to salt stress on Roi Namur,
replicated Sudan grass hay in Texas,
thirty-eight-inch baby rainbow trout
at the Esterházy-Tennessee Hatcheries.

I take her into my observatory to mark Saturn's rings,
squeeze her breast, the lens in her nipple clicks:
she has an image of Esterházy among the stars.

Agnes and Esterházy Attain Domestic Felicity
in the Corporate Suite Living Quarters

Poppy seed bread bakes in the microwave oven
for my breakfast with camomile tea.
Agnes prepares head cheese
and calf's foot jelly for Thanksgiving dinner;
a golden butterball self-basting ptarmigan waits its turn.

I check my electrolyte count as Agnes mops and scrubs,
cleans my TV screens with Endust on a cheesecloth
so from my king-size waterbed
I get clearer pictures
of the Hungary-Bulgaria soccer match.

She's an angel who sweeps through the suite
with a broom from the Lions Club broom sale.

She feeds and grooms my Dobermans,
drops barbecue into the tank for Fair-Haired Boy,
places deer mice in the glassed-in garden
for Zoltan the puff adder.

She arranges my pillows,
brings me bread and tea,

bellydances as I eat and watch Hungary
thrust home its winning goal.

A Smell of Cabbage

In a pot on my credenza
stuffed cabbage is warming.

Where did you come from? I ask.
From the old country, says Nagy,

can't you tell?
After all these years in a business office

are you able to remember
grape pickers crowding a hillside in October?

I only see my property along Lake Shore Drive,
my buildings in the Loop, I tell him.

Do you remember the taste
of homemade plum brandy? he says,

the feel of dancing
all night to gypsy music?

Nagy, I reply, you're romantic and sentimental,
that was another world.

Do you remember the wood carvings of the shepherds?
Embroideries and homespuns of the village girls?

The cabbage smell tickles my nose.
Want some? he says, serving me.

As I eat he makes palacsinta on my desk,
hums a folk tune from Matyós.

I remember summer houses and cave baths,
a smell of granaries.

It's carnival time.
Men and women

carry a yards-long horn to an icy lake,
blow until a blue forehead appears

and birds transform cold church towers
into music boxes.

Esterházy's Vienna Stopover, 1973

FOR DAVID CHORLTON

I leave the train at Meidling,
follow Schönbrunnerstrasse
toward Maria Teresa's palace.
The city's depressing in winter,
only Hungarian restaurants lend it life.
A government hygienist prowls about
collecting vapor samples.

At Hotel Schönbrunn the clerk
is reading *Stern* and drinking Gösser beer.
A guest for Herr Nagy, I announce.
Suite 200, he says, crossing himself.

I knock. The door opens, lets out
a smell of burning mugwort bark.
Nagy is naked and full of needles
from self-administered acupuncture.
Come in, he says, waxing his mustache.
I glance through the window:
a van is rushing at the hygienist.
I place my forefinger under my left eye,
tug at the lower lid,
point my free hand into the street.
Nagy nudges me aside, takes aim
through sights in the window-shade cord,
fires a shot. The van swerves,
crashes into a statue of Windischgrätz
and explodes.

They'll want you to pay for damage, I remark.
He shrugs, pours kümmel.
That's business, he says,

the hygienist is my partner.
He opens the closet door—
piled high are violins smuggled from Moscow.

Esterházy in the Hospital

Esterházy's Myelogram. Mercy Hospital. Charlotte, North Carolina.
1 P.M. February 27, 1980.

You're going to feel a mosquito bite,
the neurosurgeon says, and all
the electric eels in the world
galvanize my back.
Something cold and damp revives me—
a frog is squatting on my head.
The surgeon is consulting with someone I recognize . . .
that radiologist with comblike mustache
looks like Sándor Nagy.
Who's that other doctor? I ask the orderly
as he wheels me back to my room.
Him? That's Doctor Miller, been here fifteen years.
And the frog?
The orderly looks at me.

Laminectomy. 8 A.M. February 29.

The nurse is a mesomorph with hairy hands
that work a needle into my vein.
The operation will last about two hours, she intones,
I'm going to count down from ten.
I notice some hairs
sticking through her surgical mask.
Something damp huddles at my side.

Sándor Nagy Visits Esterházy in His Private Room. 10 P.M.
March 2.

He materializes at the foot of my bed
in a phosphorescent flash,
brings apricot liqueur and news from Moscow and Prague.
You can't stand there naked, I tell him,
so he moves to one side,
pours brandy into glasses that appear in his hand.
Are you hungry? he says, spreading caviar
on Swedish rye. They gave me
a graham cracker and milk,
I reply, and he looks sick. But recovers.
A nurse comes in followed by Sándor's frog,
stands at my side until I swallow six pills—
Sándor blends into the color TV waiting for her to leave.
Want some bone marrow? I got it from the lab.
It used to be your favorite snack, he says,
sprinkling paprika. No, I say,
you've got to go, it's past visiting hours.
The nurse screams in the hall.
Sándor shrugs, slips into a fur coat:
It's snowing in Budapest, he says.

The Return of Nagy. 10 A.M. March 3.

He's making rounds in scrub suit and surgical mask.
I thought you were in Budapest,
I thought you left last night.
He lowers the mask, uses my TV for a mirror,
clips his nose hair and mustache.
A smell of Lake Balaton invades the air;
Sasha the frog leaps from the bathroom,
corrects course in mid-flight,
plops down on my pillow.

Agh, says Sándor. Agh, Sasha replies.
Esterházy my friend, says Sándor,
you do not want us here? Then we go.
And they leave.

The Priest Arrives. 10:05 A.M.

In walks Father Brown with his plastic clip-on
Roman collar. Good morning, how're you feeling?
Do you want to receive communion?
Good morning, Father, I'm fine;
yes, I'd like communion today,
some funny things have been going on.
We say the Lord's Prayer together
and he holds the wafer out to me,
lightly sprinkled with paprika.

Christmas Eve, 1980

The boy pours my bottled water from Lourdes into the tub.
I peer through the hotel window:
Budapest evanesces behind falling snow.
The boy empties bottle after bottle.
Your bath's ready, he says.
As I take out my wallet
a figure appears in the street:
he wears a sheepskin cloak
and cap with leather appliqué;
a comblike mustache covers his lip.
I start for the door.
And your bath? the boy says.
Rebottle it, I reply, leaving a tip.

Razor-sharp footprints lead me to a sidewalk café.
Sándor Nagy sits at a table.
He snaps his fingers:
a waiter looms over us with two glasses
of Bugac bitters on a millstone
carried in the manner of a tray.
He serves us, then blends into a snowbank.
How were the mudbaths? says Nagy.
I went to Lourdes instead, I reply;
my gout was cured on the spot,
melanoma takes a little longer.
If it's cured quickly, he says,
it was only half a disease.
If it takes longer, it digs your grave.
We drink our bitters.

In some Romanesque building
violins scratch out a czardas.

Snowflakes cover Nagy's eyebrows and mustache.
I leave in the morning for Fátima, I tell him.
He smiles. If one faithful man
stands before a rock, he says, the rock may work miracles.
I start for the hotel, look back:
the table's deserted; my own footprints, gone.

Esterházy's Honeymoon

North Carolina, September 1, 1981

My first wife Agnes and I are in Greenville.
The hot line from Washington glows.
Colonel Tsung is here, says Ron,
he's attacking Pitt County with a heat wave.
The telephone melts.
The night table incinerates.

What is it, dear? You look
ashen, Agnes says, sipping kümmel
during the coitus interruptus.

Colonel Tsung is here, I reply.
Darling, she says, why don't you
fish or cut bait?

Crimea, September 2

We're still trying to honeymoon,
this time in my Black Sea dasha.
Agnes is stuffing snails into the breakfast mushrooms.
I sip subrouska.
The doorbell rings:
it's Abe Rosenstein the Naval Attaché.
Let me in, he says, I'm being tailed.
A lizard dozes on his scrambled eggs.

Come in, I reply. Want a drink?
Aquavit, he says, and I pour.
Nice dasha you've got here, he says

with a real estate broker's eye.
Talk turkey, I say, I'm on my honeymoon.

He turns on a jamming device in his NROTC ring,
scribbles on a yellow legal pad:
Colonel Tsung is here.

Come into the kitchen, meet my wife, I say,
and he follows.
I select a Sabatier bread knife,
plunge it into his chest.

Why did you do that? says Agnes.
The real Attaché, I patiently explain,
is an Academy Man.

Budapest, September 3

The Danube's not so blue as I remember it;
even here the fish mutate,
grow feet to go ashore.

Someone's following me.
An Oriental businessman slips out of the Hilton
as I kneel in Coronation Church,
follows me to Fisherman's Bastion.

We're alone.
Everyone else is at a soccer match.
We meet once more, says Tsung.
Yes, I say. Now he's wearing
a purple-green kimono that looks
like a kakemono silk painting.

Don't touch your camera, I warn him
or you're a dead man forever.
My hand's on my Maltese cross that shoots darts.

Comrade Esterházy, he smiles, I want you to meet
my aide who's been keeping tabs on you.

Agnes appears at my side.
She sinks her needle-fine
fingernails into my neck.

Therapy for Esterházy in the Temple of Asklepios

No red peppers
no apples
radishes
tomatoes
no red meat
for Esterházy the Mercenary.

Only calm blue grapes
semolina dumplings
bland rice
for three months.

I inhale vapors.
Asklepios
in the guise of a dog
licks my neck
at the edge of the whirlpool bath.

Ten Eurasian dancing girls
glide among the vineyards.
I go off with two of them.
The others
play flutes
and drums
in the dark.

Esterházy's Memoirs
February 18, 1982

Be engaged, take risks. If you lose an empire, you gain
nothing.

NAGY

The venture into the copra trade
on Roi Namur, and the Megaton
Apartment Complex at White Sands
were my undoing.

My right hemisphere has failed.
Intuitions, once plentiful
as Japanese Christmas tree lights,
have burned out. I cannot trade
my Victorian brooches for food stamps.
I subsist on unflavored gelatin.

Agnes took the files,
the Empire furniture,
the word processors,
dumped Fair-Haired Boy the piranha
and Zoltan the puff adder
into the Chicago Drainage Canal.

On the two-hundredth floor
of the Esterházy Corporate Suite
I sit on a straw mat in a corner,
writing on crumpled paper.
Birds and helicopter pilots look in.

From a secret safe beneath the mat
I remove Merovingian jewelry,
an Egyptian scarab,

a pebble from the Iron Age on which
is abraded a smiling frog.
On a moonstone which catches light and dark
appears a familiar face with a mustache.

III

from Machetes: Poems of the Mexican Revolution

La voz del pueblo, voz de Dios.
Voice of the people, voice of God.

Machetes

Bullets do not bite.
Machetes bite.
Bullets are locusts—
impersonal,
migratory.
But my machete
cuts cane,
clears brush,
is my trusted friend.
Antonio,
in the north
the land is parched,
even blood evaporates.
You made no living
from the soil,
ate only cactus pears
and rattlesnakes.
Now you come south
to Guerrero, where
fence posts take root
and blood boils
even when the sun is low.
Antonio,
the posts you sink
are on my land.
Your bullets
rust in your gun.
A red snake
uncoils from your neck.

In a Pueblo in Chiapas

I do not want your Revolution,
your Plan of This or That.
Only bring a doctor
if you come.
Worms with curved tails
eat like machetes
into the skin of children.

My baby's soul hangs from his mouth
like a thread of spittle.
The worms have swum
through his blood
into his eyes.
Already they are turning
into dark moths.

The Municipal President of Tequistalpa to Felix Díaz

The land is here
but it is gone.
You have taken it.
The spirits are yours now;
they work the land at night.
Bananas turn black as coffee,
avocados hard as faces of soldiers.
Your men have hanged the priest,
jerked me off with sandpaper
in front of women;
my member is a corncob
from which red gruel drips.
What next? Do you also
take our sons?

Pascual Orozco

I want pay for my soldiers
who have nothing to eat.
The breasts of our women
are hard and dry,
our childrens' bellies round
with the shape of the world.

You, Francisco Madero, you
and your council of ministers
have a nice time of it;
you eat tortas of head cheese,
drink myrtle juice,
sleep in beds.

The bank has not yet
turned over the money?
That is the only reason
my men must wait?

Madero,
we have been hungry a long time.
We die,
have no money for a priest,
no soap to clean ourselves.

Victoriano Huerta

His favorite drink was cognac, and the remark was made that
he considered Hennessy and Martell the only foreigners worth
knowing.

EDITH O'SHAUGHNESSY

Half a dozen fellows in an ugly mood passed in the street,
shouting "Death to Huerta!" It happens that Huerta was inside
at the time. He heard the cry, got up, and walked to the door—
alone. "Here is Huerta," he said. "Who wants him?"

ROSA KING

This Madero,
this tantrum-ridden dreamer
has no balls.
He dogs the footsteps
of presidential succession
like a dumb animal,
talks to the spirit world
from which he comes.
But now he lies
with balls of lead.
I am in command.

With my officers
I drink this country of mine,
this saloon, this bottle of cognac,
as China and Japan salute me,
my compadre Henry Lane Wilson hugs me,
the Bank of England
and Holy Mother Church
honor me by filling
my cartridge belts with money.

Villa and Zapata
assault me from the front,

Carranza and Obregón
stab me in the back;
four metallic leaves
tremble like Judas kisses.
I escape to Spain.
The country continues to seethe
and must be pacified:
I return to Texas,
am detained at Fort Bliss.
I do not feel comfortable
among smiles of gringo police.

My liver is inflamed.
A doctor I have never seen
does quick surgery,
no anesthetizing,
leaves the wound open as he departs.
I ask my daughter to sing
my favorite Mexican songs.

Twenty-five Panchos: Genovevo de la O Speaks to His Men

General Robles cannot single me out,
I look the same as you.
We dress in white pajamas.
We are all named Pancho:
Pancho 1, Pancho 2,
Pancho 3. . . .
Troops cannot catch us,
the hacienda owners cannot crush us,
we merge into corn, hide like mice,
become snakes at night.
We ambush their patrols
as they ride in single file,
twenty-five Panchos sink their fangs
into the horses' shanks,
twenty-five machetes
lop off legs like twigs.
The Zapata brothers think they run these hills,
but ask Robles, who fought the Yaqui in the north,
who is his true enemy in the south.
Ask him. He knows.
His horses have no hooves.

Zapata's Sister Speaks

Miliano, do not look for me
in Villa de Ayala.
Federal police hold me in Cuernavaca.
General Robles burns pueblos,
then visits me in jail.

Miliano,
do you nap with insects in the shade?
Is your blood turned to holy water?
I want you to bring to Cuernavaca
a river of white pajamas,
lie in wait for Robles
along the paths you know so well,
fill his throat with red coffee beans,
pierce his eyes with maguey thorns.

Then take me home.

José, Age 8

Men came on horses,
killed the dog
with rifle butts.
My father hid among trees
in the jungle.
They put my mother
on the ground
and hurt her.
She still cries.
They took the cow and hens.
Hungry, I look for caterpillars,
find bones and sandals
beneath a tree.

A Civilian Defender, Port of Vera Cruz
April 21, 1914

It was around eleven o'clock in the morning when American
marines appeared, as if from out of the bottom mud.

They are husky and blond,
they surge like lava
through a cornfield.
Women throw boiling water at them,
men load pistols, a few old rifles.
We try to retreat into shadows
like squid into ink,
present boneless targets that swim
beneath their lines of fire.
The sewing machines they bring
stitch rosebushes
into simple white clothes.

The world needs peace,
their president tells reporters,
under no circumstance
will Americans fight Mexicans.
Three hundred women and men
cannot hear his words.
Blue eyes fly like eagles
over our oilfields.
How far we are from God,
how close to the USA.

Anenecuilco: The Pueblo Speaks

True maps are drawn by naked feet.
Six hundred years
my children work the land.
Dust blows into the air,
washes away in streams,
but the feet of my children
retrace the maps.

Lawyers come with papers
which say that hacienda owners
own the land.
Soldiers come,
hang my sons from trees whose branches
should bend from the weight of mangoes.
My sons stand in line.
When all the trees are full,
soldiers line my sons against adobe walls,
and clouds of dust
blow into the air.

Green sugarcane
does not rest on Sundays.
It licks machete wounds,
grows in quiet heat.
Sugar mills rise like pyramids,
hacienda owners and lawyers
lie with my daughters
in Sunday heat.

You talk of God in many ways,
my fellow generals,
but when we know so little
we ought to hold our tongues.
I believe that God exists;
if he did not,
death with its lizard face
would be free from judgment,
and the Revolution would be
a crown of cartridge belts.
Bolder words have come
from men more clever than I,
but like the iguana that falls
to the river from its tree,
men vanish.

Andrea Mendoza Is Aboard the Train from Durango

Your father forbids you to see me again.
In my veins I bear
ten dark drops of Indian blood.
I sold smoked minnows
in a market stall in Michoacán.
Now I am a captain,
I ride for Lázaro Cárdenas.

Your father brings you by train
to a convent in the capital.
Soldiers with machine guns ride on top.
With unseen machetes my men climb aboard,
prune the soldiers from the roof,
stop the train in the desert.

Come with me, Andrea,
or two hundred passengers will be shot.
I will let your father live
to remember this trip
one way or the other.

Lázaro Cárdenas

In the mountains of Morelos,
Zapata, I have seen you.
The bullets in your body
have become dust
but you are everywhere.

I come from Jiquilpan.
My father farmed a plot of rocks,
I brought water on my shoulder.
Now they have made me president
of bright lights
under which people read.

But in my pueblo
no one reads.
Not even the stars are bright;
each one stands for a baby
who did not live
to learn to read.

I will rule the nation
from Jiquilpan,
farm this plot of rocks
with patience.
Even in meager furrows
corn can grow.

Miguel Pro, S.J., Faces a Calles Firing Squad

Bullets, I look for you,
stand up for you,
am not worthy to receive you,
but only say the word
and I shall be healed.

Saint Paul says
all things serve and cooperate
for the good of those who love God.
Bullets, I pray
you cooperate with Calles
for my good.

I have worked among
the poorest of the poor.
On this head of mine
not worth three centavos
the Calles government has a price.
This day I shall taste
honey on my tongue.

Bullets, mark well your way.
Be as hard with me
as I am delicate with you,
for you shall die
and I shall live.

Otilia Colunga on Her Knees in Line
Outside the Basilica of the Virgin of Guadalupe

Bits of gravel
bite my flesh.
I kneel in blood
which is not my blood.
Someone behind me
kneels in mine.
The way is slow,
the virgin, far.
On my head
the sun is a crown
of maguey thorns.
Bus fare from Toluca
took my savings—
I must give
my other sixty centavos
to the virgin
to help her in her work
among the poor.
A vender is vending
orange juice
outside the fence,
one peso a glass.
The virgin
will ease my thirst,
help me find work,
help me buy food
for my children
in Toluca.
The virgin, who lives
above the cool moon,
will hear my prayers.

IV

from Culpepper of the Low Country

In the course of a day's fishing it will often happen
that some fish are landed while others get away.

ROBERT W. WHITE
The Abnormal Personality

Culpepper Goes Bass Fishing

The live oak branch bends
on hinges. Charles Tucker
Cauthen Culpepper takes a swig
of Rebel Yell and gets down.

He's going fishing for bass—
follows pig tracks to the lake,
kicks a copperhead out of the way,
picks a lure, casts into the mist.

Hushed voices talk around him.
Old friends come near.
Boy, says his father's voice,
it's time you got a belt
for them britches,
your belly's gettin so fat
it's gonna fall and crush your balls.

All day he fishes. Drinks Rebel Yell.
Packs his lures. Goes back
to the tree. Walks up the branch.
Disappears.

Culpepper Redeemed

He emerges from the First Foursquare
Church of the Divine Apogee,
saved forever from sin,
corruption, the Devil and Rebel Yell.

Two hours renascent,
he springs into his new being.
Singing and clapping resound in his ears;
the laying of hands like a mighty current
sweeps away his thirst, his sins,
corruption. With magnetic force
it soaks up the Holy Spirit.

Sin, go 'way. Devil, git back.
Culpepper's done with you,
he's on the Holy Track.

Singing and clapping,
clapping and singing.
Culpepper and the Devil
ain't friends no more.

A Moment in Time at Culpepper Plantation

Flowering plums and dogwoods
flank the approach to the house.
It's past midday—servants
are gathered in a rear grove
slowly eating sweet potatoes.
Insects doze in the shade.

Six Grecian columns
support a double-decked portico.
Infant Culpepper sits
between two bronze lions
drinking a potation of wine.

The central hall inside is cool;
air currents and hushed voices
circulate around Clara Cauthen Culpepper,
who listens for news from Charleston,
a shawl on her shoulders for sudden chills:

    . . . the Stephen Boykins
    of Mount Pleasant
    entertained a guest
    from London who declared,
    I do bethink myself at home,
    so regally am I treated . . .

    . . . Langston Hodding
    Carter Cuttino,
    formerly of Mississippi,
    has given up reading law
    to devote himself full time

to rice planting
in the low country . . .

Clara Cauthen Culpepper's wine glass is empty.
Servants don't respond to her calls.
She steps outside, takes the decanter
from Infant Culpepper's hands,
returns to her proper station
among air currents in the hall.

Uncle Max Steeps Young Culpepper in Local Tradition as They Work and Drive

They're loading fatback
on the white Toyota pickup truck.
Morning beats like a slow heart.
The rest of the day is an upright loom
with threads of sun and Spanish moss.

We cultivate mushrooms in moonlight, says Max,
make wine by south wind,
sip milk from poinsettia stalks.

We belong to the old days
of spicebush tea and yellow jacket soup.
Flint corn stood silky as the afternoon.

Culpepper sees a lizard.

When it puffs its throat
into a balloon, says Max,
bite off its head before its tongue
coats your mouth with mucus.

They head for the packing house.

Slow down, says Max,
there's a gray cat on the road.
Stop the truck, get out and stick him good
or we've got bad luck clear to town.

See how that burned plantation
settles to the ground.
Go slow, see how everywhere

water in the creeks doesn't flow,
and cows rest on their ribs.

The fatback is full of moving things.
A cock crows in the dark over Charleston.

We've got to wait,
says Max. We can't go on,
we can't go back. Bad luck to turn around—
and this morning we washed our faces
in the same swamp.

The Squirrel

Culpepper's eating goobers
on a cypress stump.
Vines and snakes curl around him.
On his way home from a hog calling,
he's stopped for goobers and sweet taters.

He shot a squirrel
but it's for supper
with water lily seeds
and jessamine roots.

He's carrying it on his belt,
remembers suddenly a trip he made
with Uncle Max when he was six
to Great Dismal Swamp to see
cockfights, sees instead
a rodent's face
as it's eaten by a snake.

He pulls the squirrel from his belt,
leaves the tiny body on the stump.

Uncle Max Leaves for Rumania

He eats sweet tater custard for the last time,
gives Culpepper a gold bangle for his wrist,
camel bells for his marsh-tackey pony.

Never hunt the snowy owl, he says,
that flies from pine to pine.
Don't ever fish for copper-nose bream
or their dark red spots
reappear in your eyes.

A Negro girl serves him syrup of figs
from a decanter, disappears inside.

Your sweet mother never squeezed
lemon into clam soup, Max goes on,
she saved the spines
of warmouth perch for pins.

He sips blood balm laced with Rebel Yell.

Don't chase deer into the sea.
They swim out of sight, nose out of water;
the venison then is flavorless,
only the nose fit to eat.

Culpepper jots down everything on a yellow legal pad.
Max gets up,
embraces the boy. Take care, he says,
have a good day, goes out
to his long-backed mare, rides away
through wild orange trees.

Culpepper and the Public Health Physician

The doctor moves his fingers
to opposite sides. They disappear.
Culpepper watches. Doc, he says,
they're gone. Yes, the doctor concedes,
I know. I studied for this.
And now young man,
can you count backward from 100 by sevens?
Sure, Culpepper says, that'd be fun,
but I came to tell you Alberta's in pain.
Do you know what day it is? the doctor says.
Sure do, Culpepper alertly responds, but
Alberta's all excruciated. . . .
What does "A stitch in time" mean?
Doc, she's hurtin' bad, she'll need
a lot more than one.
Can you close this safety pin?
Them's for diapers, I got no babies,
it's Alberta needs to see you.
All right, bring her in next Thursday.
Doc, she met a bear in the berry patch,
would like to see you now.

An Outing on Pawley's Island

Like a sturgeon leaping out of the water,
turning somersaults,
Culpepper swims twice around the island,
bolts ashore,
does two hundred push-ups,
suns himself on a palmetto log
with a glass of sherry.
A Negro girl appears, on her head
a tureen of seafood gumbo.
She stands on russet pine straw
near him as he dines.
Don't slurp the soup, she says.
He grows rigid, slowly gets to his feet,
a long whip in his hand.
Marse Culpepper, she cries.
The whip's report is a rifle shot—
a rattler's head falls at her feet.

Alberta Abrams Fishes for Mullet

The planks and posts are rotten.
She imagines the landing
collapses—she sinks—
her lungs fill with water and silt;
Culpepper comes in his white canoe,
pulls her out, rushes her home
in his white Toyota pickup truck,
waits in the parlor
as the doctor tends her,
sees himself in the ten-foot mirror,
rubs his feet on the Turkish rug,
sits awkwardly on the Empire sofa,
admires dolls and daguerreotypes
in the corner cabinet. The doctor
comes downstairs. There was
nothing I could do, she hears him say.

Reunion

Culpepper and twelve Negroes
carry fat pine torches and long switches,
make their way among twenty-foot cane
with corn sacks full of coots and bats
for breakfast.

A long-backed mare outside the meat shack
is eating sugar yams.
Culpepper bursts inside.
There's Uncle Max in tall silk hat,
face pitted with pox,
nose full of blue veins,
eating cornflakes.

How was Rumania? Culpepper asks.
Full of generals, plague and politicians, says Max,
so I came back to God's country.
He pours more cereal
into fresh mare's milk.

Sir Gander-Puller of the Low Country

Richly mounted on a stallion
Uncle Max stole from gypsies,
Culpepper appears at the head of the course,
his hardware refulgent with Rally cream wax.

A featherless gander richly greased
is suspended over the course.
With celerity must Culpepper
astride his charging horse dispatch
such squirming matter as hand may encounter
at end of lubricous neck.

Sir Knight, says a pimply herald,
Beefeater Gin on his breath,
art thou disposed to battle
yon cockatrice whose claws disembowel,
whose stench cometh from below?

Turn me loose, Culpepper cries
and with a Johnny Reb yell to unman the bird
passes full tilt beneath the target,
grabs the gander in his gauntlet,
jerks off the head.
Full six such trials does Culpepper pass,
six ganderheads does he amass.

He salutes the gallery,
rides before Lady Alberta,
she of the camellia-white thighs,
stiffens his lance,
dubs her Queen of Love and Beauty.

She proclaims him Sir Gander-Puller,
promises to play later
the fatal game of hearts.

Bloodworms

Alberta's scared to death of them,
says they get that way from sucking fingers,
won't touch them for love or lucre.

Culpepper's digging them up on the tidal flats
to fish for flounder,
puts them in an ice chest with seaweed.

They row in his white canoe to Stede Bonnet's ship,
half submerged like a forgotten chum pot,
climb aboard and rig for fishing.

He separates the worms.
With cutlass-like nippers
they'd like to slit each other's throats.

Alberta shudders daintily. How grotesque
and baroque, she says, as she slips
squirming baby copperheads onto her hooks.

Culpepper Is Politicized

Senator Ravenel Tillman Legare's
giving a major speech
in front of the Winn Dixie store.

We must reverse the trend, he says,
of everything that's going on.
The state needs a one-crop economy,
full employment in the fields.
Ship Jane Fonda back to Hanoi,
A-rabs back to Suddy-Rabia.
We need pecan pie and motherhood.

Culpepper's deeply moved.
Something stirs in his chest.
He's ready to march
to the thump of his tachycardia.

Near the Ocean, Culpepper Lies in State

Mosquitoes and fleas are motionless;
Venus's-flytraps, numb.

He lies among gomo roots,
surrounded by Trappist monks.
Blackwater fever finished him,
The Great Octopus
has pulled him to its beak.

Forming a human pyramid
on his white Toyota pickup truck,
twelve Negroes sing a dirge in Gullah.

Mournfully munching cracklin's,
Sweet Alberta sits beneath a faded banner
marked Spoon Bread Festival Queen.
Poor darlin', she sobs, he'll never again
buy Slim Jims for breakfast at the Seven-Eleven Store,
sip Catawba Red from the apple juice bottle,
pour salt on slugs in the early dew.

His mother fans herself on a sack of pine bark chips,
calls to remembrance
her wine-swigging infant son.
He made his bid for life, she thinks,
and now to peat moss he returns.

High on a cypress branch, Uncle Max
hides his thoughts in sour mash.

A red sky attends the end of day,
sailors stand stiffly at attention

at the Charleston Naval Base.
Muffled rounds are fired from Fort Sumter.
Fort Moultrie slips
a little farther into the sand.

Other Titles in the Contemporary Poetry Series